Jew's Harp

poems by

Walter Hess

D1738595

Jew's Harp

poems by

Walter Hess

Pleasure Boat Studio: A literary Press
New York

Jew's Harp
Poems by Walter Hess, ©2010

ISBN 978-1-929355-63-1
Library of Congress Control Number: 2009940410

Design by Jason Schneiderman
Artwork by Herb Stern

Pleasure Boat Studio is a proud subscriber to the Green Press Initiative. This program encourages the use of 100% post-consumer recycled paper with environmentally friendly inks for all printing projects in an effort to reduce the book industry's economic and social impact. With the cooperation of our printing company, we are pleased to offer this book as a Green Press book.

Pleasure Boat Studio books are available through the following:
SPD (Small Press Distribution) Tel. 800-869-7553, Fax 510-524-0852
Partners/West Tel. 425-227-8486, Fax 425-204-2448
Baker & Taylor 800-775-1100, Fax 800-775-7480
Ingram Tel 615-793-5000, Fax 615-287-5429
Amazon.com and bn.com

and through
PLEASURE BOAT STUDIO: A LITERARY PRESS
www.pleasureboatstudio.com
201 West 89th Street
New York, NY 10024

Contact Jack Estes
Fax; 888-810-5308
Email: pleasboat@nyc.rr.com

Acknowledgements

"Survivor" appeared in *The New Vilna Review,* as well as in *Jewish Currents*

"Oma" was included in the anthology, *Blood to Remember: American Poets on the Holocaust*

"Children's Drawings" first appeared in *Barrow Street*

"Daughter," "Poem: My political program," and "Poem: the old hag says" appeared in *The American Poetry Review*

"Some Jewish Poets of Medieval Spain - A Ghazal" appeared in *Mima'amakim*

FOR HANNAH

Though stumbling about with my small humm
in all this mumbling to myself, my dear,
I felt the lake's fine evening silence thrum;
the moon's wide casting alb greet Algol and Altair.
You see, I've gone to space, to earth, the past,
sometimes our kids, and kissed their cheeks in line,
yet never, though I often wanted, cast
your deserving, into measure, into rhyme.
Why that neglect? Why dodge? How could that be?
Unless my soul believed so very long,
knew years ago, of that impossibility
to parse your goodness, sweetness into song.
I'll try again though all my limits show.
Still, who needs verse? It's what our clasped hands know.

Contents

Survivor

It took some time
to look at all those pictures,
the black and white ones;
to hear those stories once again;
heads nodding toward
her and him;

that book of shadows
when we were kids
who knew enough
to fill in that which happened;
knew to perfection that desire,
no, the need to stay apart,
away from them;

from that which happened
endlessly to those you loved
but not to you.

OMA

1.

She stayed in the village where they knew her worth —
sixteen and pregnant and no one reproached her.

2.

Once I saw the gypsy at her door,
skin like oil and beads of coral about her neck,
who looked in my Oma's eyes, and bowed her head,
who saw her sorrows but the muted flint of fiery being;
her joy, long flowing silence and calm knowing.

We sat in front of bread and butter then —
mothers and grandmothers rising like steam
from sweet creamy coffee,
safety like raisins among the blue-lined china
and the nougat fathers dotted along the four o'clock napery.

This is for my grandmother, an unimportant Jew,
whose apron gathered morels in a green pine wood,
who, in a walled city, died of Typhus
in Tereszin, city of Therese, Empress of Typhus,
eight days before the liberating Russian army came.

Bulldozers may have shoveled her to stuff the pits,
to stem the stench and sickness
from leaping beyond sane and certain borders,

laconic hands on throttles, shovels,
levers doing overtime,
thin arms,
heads falling back in awkward postures.

There must have been some scraping sound of gears
of metal on the hard-baked ground
of the resistance so much poundage makes
against an oily diesel energy.

Or, she just fell over, toppled in a heap,
became a boulder,
a holy stone,
one of many dotting the parade ground
before which even the dark tanks halted –
steel-tinged with the awesome soul of so much stone.

I think that someone picked her up,
a Russian soldier maybe,
persuaded beyond her rotting flesh
by memory and awe to place her gently with the others,
to burn with others in the immense hollow of her grave.
In other words, in piety, doing what I do now.

Grandmother,
the cantillation of the rails
whistles in the three-starred night,
enfilades where I am not;
and where I am, the song evokes distance, borders, margins,
winds of cloves, dark whistling winds
bearing cinnamon and plaited candles;
Sabbath ends reflected in the half moon of your nails
and both your hands upon my shoulder resting.
What do you know about me?

I shine like cobbles after rain, dew on a web,
Friday nights,
and I've seen wonders:
eyes, chins –

sadness like yours —
song, speech, love, all like yours.

And you, gathered like weed with serrate leaves,
like potato vines piled high for burning.
I ride a train whose rolls of dust...

I am not here —
almost.

Sometimes
I hear your great haloo within the loamy wood.
Come
gather where the mushroom grows in oblique golden light,
where folded hills, where sun,
where brilliant semaphores of leaves
leave signal echoes along the lakeside road

and they are lovely.

CHILDREN'S DRAWINGS

The colors of Terezin
have eyes that never sleep,
contain blue thorn and wire thorn,
red sun of Moloch fire.

The colors of Terezin
have eyes that never sleep,
blue thorn and wire thorn
that pierce the pupil.

The colors of Terezin
have eyes that never sleep,
red sun,
Moloch and Haephestus fire
that hammer razors,
slashing open lids,
the nictitating membranes of the brain
and all the networks of forgetting.

HAIMAT

Walking,
the boy saw:

The moon in a slot of sky
between the roofs of two houses.

Metal cobbles like shiny
backs of beetles – pieces of armor in a
book.

A yellow leaf shaped like
a heart or the tip of a spear flown
up against the steel-gray sky.

A house that showed a corner
of shattered masonry;
thin mud-colored bricks.

On the white walls of a house,
black lines.

Behind the calcimined walls,
pictures of fish swallowing
their tails.

The blank faces of the houses
and the cylindrical trees.

His hands held feeling
like the orange light of a candle
in a narrow room.

This was 1937 or '38.

1938

Near the yard,
noon flies.

I held his hand
and the golden buzz
of the sun.

His hand.

The black silk muzzle
of our cows,
odor of sour milk,
cock flapping on the midden,
the barn's dusty lintel,
and the fine gray web.
Meadow tracks dry
of the morning mud,
the forget-me-nots.

His hand.

See there the silver
and high distant marvel
drawing lines straighter
than the corner of my house
murmuring
en route to Godesberg.

Who is this Chamberlain
who splits the morning,
who sits and chooses
where I love
the silver river line?

Not the black halo only
about the distant
flashing drone.
But I knew well
the cow,
familiar,
in the shadow of the great pear tree,
was gone
forever.

His hand.

1940 – In the Heart of the Andes

It is amazing how long they last –
winter and Sabbath silence,
aprons,
Opa's blessing,
Manasse and Ephraim –
compañeros de mi Vida,
adios Muchachos.

Andean bells in silent office,
cross-clangors sweeping
into half-remembered streets
cross Chimborazo switchbacks.

How black yet sleek the engines
silver the rails,
how smoke fills space,
the filling odor of burning coal,
the many oranges of Riobamba,
rich platanos,
the offering of silent ponchos, maroon and ochre,
and on the terrace of the great Machachi church
where baroque tiers
attempt to outface brilliant Cotopaxi,
where once great Inca offered bloody hearts,
her black robes ruffled,
cold blows the wind from Cotopacxi,
the ancient woman screams,
"Judio! Judio!"

and Chino, my friend
in the valley of the Andes,
walks with me,
hands me half his Chiremoya
and only half in play,

we spit the pits of luscious fruit
in long and cheerful arcs
out onto the Royal road.

Opa – The Old Synagogue

The house in which we bowed toward the door
   L'cho Daudi
where carpets softly caught our sweets
   L'cho Daudi
I want it back
   L'cho Daudi
though others own it now.

Hewn stone, I marvel yet,
   square as the adze could make it;
the songs of morning, evening, night;
   the sacrifices at their proper hour
were shot while trying to escape.
   L'cho Daudi

The house
   wherein you celebrated sacrifices
is now another's,
   the stones tooled to a solid beauty
hard like a tower
   L'cho Daudi
can't have it back,
must sing in other places now,
   L'cho Daudi.

ELISHA'S PRAYER

So he departed thence, and found Elisha the son of Shaphat, who was plowing, with twelve yoke of oxen before him, and he with the twelfth; and Elijah passed over unto him, and cast his mantle over him. (1 Kings 19:19)

What I have is what I have been given.
What I ask is to remember:
chimney and chair and furrow;
all the cold mornings and the oxen's
breath;
the pond's thin ice in winter and
the refracting shards;
and all my oxen's names, the twelve that
fed the multitude.

When taking my sharp knife to all
their throats,
the knife I had been whetting
all these years,
I saw the mountain break, and heard
the oxen bellow,
heard the children's smacking lips,
 the thunder from afar,
stillness, and the blazing wind; your work,
your work, oh God.
Let me remember that – my parents' faces
and the oxen's bellowing.

On First Looking into Fagles' Homer

Be kind to travelers, strangers.
The woman on the corner speaking German,
small children in tow and paper in hand,
looking, "Please..."

The thin man at the station,
starched white shirt, sweating,
holding tight his wicker suitcase
and in Creole says, "Where..."

The confused old lady with the pocketbook
and the flowered dress
standing at the candy store:
"Is this..."

Remember, that in days of old,
Angels and Gods descended,
came down as humans dressed like you or me,
and you never knew to whom you spoke.
So Ulysses in the middle sea
and Jacob on Mesopotamian roads...

and Rachel smiles.
Manoah sees into the distance.
And a man comes ...

A woman in a wheelchair,
she carries a quart of milk...

All wanderers are sacred
to the God of guests.

A Midrash on Genesis 23

Old Satan came to Sarah saying,
Sarah, say, where is your son?
He's on the mountain three days gone.
He's up there on the mountain, praying

with his father who is teaching
how to offer sacrifice.
Using sheep to do the office,
mountain rams, and God beseeching.

Now Sarah, Sarah, are you certain
that it won't be Isaak gets the call,
won't be Isaak on that altar
won't be Isaak's final curtain?

Sarah, disbelieving, full of fear,
rushed to Shaishi the great giant.
You are tall, you are reliant,
you see far, you are a seer.

Then at Sarah's sharp insistence,
Shaishi, with his long-range vision
saw Moriah with precision,
told her what was in the distance:

One old man, and there's a youth
upon the altar. Cords are wound.
And that youth is being bound.
Shaishi, say, is that the truth?

Is that the truth? The mother cried,
It is my very dear son's life.
The old man's hand contains a knife.

It's there and then that Sarah died.

STEPHANIE'S QUESTION

"Suppose you weren't here. Would I be here?
Suppose that like your Opa you had...?"
A shadow slickered down her face, a fear
that stopped. She then edged closer to my side
and took my hand as if to solace me.

He held my hand when I was Stephie's age.
Praise and instruction in our step, we walked
a rhythm like the singing of a page
of psalms in Shul. Call and response. We talked.
He held my hand and solaced me.

Dear Steph, Survivors have no other task
than being who and what they are. You ask
what you already know. You are where you are meant to be.
Your very question solaced me.

DAUGHTER

she sails so far away
no wind but some initial
impetus when we first walked
and rocked
her crying back to peace
guides her
or so I pride myself

my shoulder beach
her head a sea
(moon and a silent ebbing)
a shifting border and
most perfect joining
building at noon or in
the star-fled morning
oh such a lovely city
to which she sails

or so I pride myself

About Time

Inside my son plays Miles;
outside the lake grows gray.
The woods – an oily green that says
go home.
I hear Chopin, Scriabin;
bass and piano like the darkening wood.
Then Davis with this longing blues,
a yearning gleaned from light.
The dark wood yields a hollow longing –
flute and harp, some Mozart sounds.

The gray breaks up.
Blue threads the clouds, the sky,
a mottled light out on the deck.

Down here there are no colors of our own.
I only see what the changing sky allows –
the sky amends both lure and longing.

I held him once.
Hard for me to say
that Miles is Mozart.
But I listen.

Walking Zoe to Sleep

How to negotiate transitions
from wake to sleep, from sleep
to waking is the trick. Position's

determining. And that's a truth that's deep
embossed in cheek and shoulder, bone and flesh.
I now remember how to look and keep

alert to that loud crabbing in the creche.
And long before, the fine high chirping trill,
the thrashing arms, the bouncing legs; so fresh

the tunes, so long forgot. And then the thrill,
when bending down with arms outstretched, to see
returning arms stretched out again. The will

goes numb. The daughter says, *She's got to sleep.*
Thinks, *Sometimes Dad's more trouble than he's worth.*
He's here to play and not to help. My deep

experience held somewhat cheap. Despite the dearth
of confidence Zoe's head now joins my shoulder.
We stately step as if Antaeus joining earth.

A look aslant. We tread parquet. I hold her.
We weave in dance to Artie Shaw.
Beguines begin; we wander farther, yonder,

where donkeys serenade, stars dust and glow;
deep purple moons *chantez les bas*, oh, sweet
and lovely...*the cheek of night bends gray and low,*

Lids founder, crease, enfold those eyes so black and blessed.
She's out. And daughter's scoffing too is put to rest.

Bat Mitzvah – Portion Noah

The drowned souls:

When the springs roared up,
the floods through the riven abyss
then opened as well
all the windows of heaven.

The drowned children:

no foothold below
and the throat-choking waters
and all the drowned mothers
inhaling the water
though it might have been gas.

Then died every life that had
breath in its nostrils excepting
that silent good man
who walked with his God.

So she stood in the pulpit,
this thirteen-year-old,
contending with God
like Jacob and Moses,
this covenant's daughter,
and she asked, no, demanded
to know who was just
though he call up the dawn
and show morning its place.

Wrapped in that shawl –
the shawl of the drowned
woven four fathers back–

spoke of seed time and harvest,
the unfinished God,
the wind, the dove,
and the sprig of olive.

To Allie

who wanted a poem

Memory fills the distance between
here and there; the miles apart
and the long year's gap.
And hints of joy instructing memory
to fill up chinks in space and time.
Not just your joy alone
when three-year legs raced forward
from my hands to museum glass,
where yellow quartz,
where amethyst and amber,
where diamonds, hematite and pearls
sparkled like your face.
And memory of sparkling Tuesday mornings
that filled our walking ten blocks up
to Barnes and Noble where you first
started to inhale those sparkling books.

Nevertheless,
I now wave *ciao* to memory,
joy though it brings to stuff in mind.
Stuff in mind is all it is. As the old guy
said, *The past is nothing
and we're in love with it.* Much better
to look forward. To many meetings
over and over again in many places,
Chicago and New York
and at the lake which surely sparkles now
like those old jewels and that face I love.

Some Jewish Poets of Medieval Spain – A Ghazal

Yet in the womb David told poems, a womb like Andaluz.
Still, they looked East, to David's City, ecstatic, even in Al Andaluz.

Poor, humble, brilliant Ibn Ezra, with your shirt like a sieve,
did I see you on a dirty corner on Grand Street, or was it, prophetic,
          in Al Andaluz?

Dunash: No one knows how you died. Poetic radical,
you tried, succeeded, using Arab models for your Hebrew verse, exilic,
          in Al Andaluz.

In the height of heaven, right near the throne is your abode,
oh, Ibn Abitur. I know you'd weep now, as then you wept, tragic,
          in Al Andaluz.

Khalfon, you have it right. The high and mighty send you cheese,
and just a slice, when all you want is drink. *Shver zu sein a Yid.* Comic,
          in Al Andaluz.

Shmuel: Prince, commander of Muslim Armies, Rabbi,
statesman, poet. You knew your alphaic pen was mightier than any sword
          in al Andaluz.

Who can hold you in just two lines, Judah Halevy, you
who praise God, the washerwoman, and Zion still? Now, as then, heroic
          in Al Andaluz.

Melville Crossing Madison Square

In September of 1867 Herman Melville found his oldest son dead of a self-inflicted pistol-shot. The year before, eleven years after his last fiction was badly received, Melville took the oath of office as Inspector of Customs at the Port of New York. Every morning, six days a week, he would walk from his home at 104 East 26 Street down to the docks on Gansevoort Street.

... but where did he get the gun ... ?

I had been stabbed too often ... my books I mean;
I felt it in the flesh, why not this stab?
Ah, Lizzie, Lizzie... My shoulder aches.
Our Malcolm cold and blue; his oaken door in splinters.

Down 5th Avenue

This polar wind, these birds of prey, they hover over me.
My evil art that raised a monster – who else but me?
No glistening now, or then, of yellow on the twelve-month seagull,
this plummeting Dutch darkness – in me? In him?
Dark patches fell on him; the dark threw patches down on me.
I will go pilgriming forever; knees over broken glass.

... where did he get the gun?

Across 14ᵗʰ Street

All my labor was but distraction of a troubled conscience.
Rembrandt's shadows and Turner's fog were leaven,
scant yeast for children's bread.
I wrote to buy tobacco – did he know?
Shabby clothes and insufficient food is what I gave them;
cold lodgings in the icy rooms of heaven and
small opportunities for pleasure here on earth,

when all I wanted was white clover,
perfume from Greylock thrown their way.
How Milton's daughters cursed him in his presence.

... my gun.

Down Hudson Street

Once, in Jerusalem, I stood by Shepherd's Gate,
Right on the spot where Christ was stoned, and watched
the shadows sliding sled-like down the hill of Zion
into the valley of Jehoshaphat. Then, after resting,
creep up the side of Olivet, entering tomb after tomb
and cave after cave. God overawes with silence.

... I'll call him Captain Vere

Onto Gansevoort Street

The customs house: for nineteen years an anxious harbor
for nonentities.
But the odor of hemp, of brine, of rotting wood, of tar.
Tides running in on scrolls of silver, wrecks run aground,
the sound of bells; I see the sky's reflection in the water
the shimmering rack of beams dazzle my eyes; the fine
centrifugal spokes of light around my head in sun-lit water,
glories are strung like beads; salt water is like wine.

....when they put the rope on Billy's neck, he'll cry out,

God bless Captain Vere.

Late February

This day light see-saws,
shifting cool-centered pearl
to silver.
This day,
warm orange
etches shadows
over the blooming stone.

On 94th street,
tough city sycamores
consider buds,
and the black cramping arc
of winter's haggishness.

Rooted in rivers,
the mild and cranial sky
grows large,
lifts edge to center,
embraces the silent cirrus ligatures
that mirror the cold cracking
of the river noon.

The sky just blows away.

Far down the block,
Peter, my friend,
stands,
head tipped toward the roofs,
to the fine brawling song
cascading down
of sparrows among the eaves.

In April

praise, praise in an evil world
the Hallel sung

it sings the dark,
light unannounced,
hears daunting sirens
on Columbus,
refuses to compete,
resumes
when cops or engines
warble blocks away.

Mostly, among the brownstones,
I hear the sparrows.
Their morning roar below the eaves
evokes
among the tense and hardly sleeping
the chafe of sidewalks' mica glints.

Who is this singer then, of dew,
who turns the new moon into song,
its heart
the flute and flutter of its throat,
who sings the hook-beaked kestrel
soaring
high above the Reservoir,
whose pure and uninflected nigun
sings
praise upon praise
into the baffled beauty of the light,
its liquid changes on the text?

Praise upon praise.

I may yet be his congregant.

After Labor Day

Wind, a burin,
lightly sets against the lake.
Sun strokes the pines,
my scapula.
Dark gradations steal over water.
(Rembrandt)

A distant shutter drops
(Teal in a string)
echoes to the early dusk.

On the dock my lovely son
sits,
intent,
working on a toenail.

Under the graying sky,
water,
deep shadows,
weed,
houses along the shore,
the great sun itself
take on the colors
that belong to them.

The House in April

1.

My house borders on an eight-mile lake.
Beyond the sedge,
water laps shingle and mussel shell.

The hills' firm rounding bears the sun,
the ice beneath black cedar branches;
they bend beneath the evening light,
blend silver down the valley's sloping course,
down to the mallows,
catkins,
down to the lily beneath the water.

2.

The land is priced in inches,
as cemeteries are.
I smile,
thinking of my father,
us in another country
when he and I drove cows together -
dawn coming up,
the long macadam luminous -
to market.

Poem

my political program
requires
that the shine comes off cars
and photographs and faces

abolish mirrors
quiet water is the best for combing
yet take care

(the stream Narcissus kissed is everywhere)

formica will be matte
marble will not be polished
the copper tints or the
blue glass of curtain walls
will be replaced by wood or masonry
stucco remains a problem

and we will need warehouses
vast reserves of dust and sand
carborundum
and everything
abrasive

Washington Heights – The Hudson's Edge

A small sun sets beyond the Palisades
Crimson streamers
Clouds surprising for such a sun
Run like a banner toward the Amboys
Negligent floes on the torpid river
Pile
Break up about the concrete bases of the bridge

Gulls forage
Ride
Circle and edge
Glide in their search
On palms of warming updrafts

Far on the Jersey side
The angled roofs of factories
Seem to bear old and ashen snow
Facing the water
We sit on rocking playground swings
Quiet
Not ready to go home

Black grumpy river
Or is it me
Or is it condominiums
That press down hard upon the Palisades

Now,
The wind wrapped bridge
moves against clouds
Listen
The tires
And the metal clang
Like bells
Like bells

Flight to Miami

Good lord
let sunshine spread in the sunshine state,
let fat and vitamin D stain the peninsula to gold ,
let health gush, flow to the shelter
of the gentle saint down to intensive care
where Dad has lain these long, long weeks,
more than the six he endured in Dachau

Father Jacob, father of Joseph, wrestler with life
on the far river side, sharpie,
stretch out your hand, help,
tandem against the awful knife of the dark angel;
he is not weak and no mean batter,
week after week standing with Rocca
and Beau Jack,
the farm boy without bull, lumbering
up stairs,
ten gallons flat and benzene cans.

It's true he plastered over cracks –
"let no one say the world is bad" –
but he could mix the colors of the rainbow
and knew the difference
between Zampa and Don Giovanni

BEDSIDE

From the soft moss of morning
and its stainless dew we came.
His body seemed strong,
a bare-chested wrestler.

I thought of Plato, wrestler
in the middle sea,
some chunky youth archaic and ageless:
hands slap at muscles massaging flesh.
He was pink with care

and all his organs were outside his body.
He rested on plastic and steel
in this figuration,
an insect in Devonian jungles,
beauty in its vast future.

Pus, blood, and urine in plastic bags,
the blood of unknown brothers
sinking deep into tissue (soft
moss of morning and the air stained green
by the sea).
The bellows rose and fell.
Sweet sisters monitored the dials
and I could not tell the difference
between acceptance and cold fear.

I thought of Jacob,
wrestler on the far river's side,
who took a name,
a draw,
a lifelong limp.
I thought of Jacob
on Mesapotamian roads.

He was never stronger.
His bare chest pink,
hair combed and white
and wavy.

A tube in his throat.

AT THE CEMETERY

Refugee among the stones,
poplar and holly,
earth and clay,
in one more city
searching out the comfort of a name,
an Address,
inside a neighborhood of granite.

Searching among stones,
a neighborhood in fragments.
There is no settling of scores,
no judgments.
Mourning seems simple,
just gossip,
an inventory,
groceries you have or need,
a list of green and yellow,
of tones and dances.

You gathered stones.
The rain swept by.
Sunlight swept the wind
as at the border of a sea.

You tuck the stones in at the edges.
Your practiced hand sweeps the clods gently,
even,
like pulling a blanket
up
under the chin of your friend.

Juggling Practice

Lately
I've picked up
juggling.
Not picked,
but somehow taken to the heft
of first one ball,
a weight upon three fingers
lifting shy lines toward my brow.

Two plot-evolving angles, as planes
of happy possibility practice upon the rote
of muscle and ply the distance of an eye
over the mind's geometry.
Two stitch the body's measure of the void near fingertips.

Three balls weave spider lines, a cradle gift of geometric fountains,
Pythagorean, lilting, dancing in multiple dimensions, dextrous, tripping,
sly.

Sometimes
I
d
r
o
p
a
ball,

and then I think
how I'll,
seamless, and with sleight of grace,
incorporate the error in the act.

That's to be practiced next

POEM

1.

The old hag says
unless you have experience
or
a good map
avoid shortcuts

2.

Sometimes I have words
that are unstrung
but pleasant and skipping
(buttons whirling like
flaming wheels — domestic prophesies)

3.

Sitting on the last step,
my daughter whirls a button
on a string
while the cat sleeps

4.

Old poets sing the same for everyone,
strange —
so do the young ones.
White wings beat inside my head.
The notions are confused, and
the old hag says
she'll stay away
until I stop competing.

Amaryllis

Our amaryllis appears at peculiar times,
early January, late November;
whenever it decides the time is good. And cold.
This says its birth was southern, equatorial;
that everything it knows is habited
by the hard reason of its roots,
and to that core of starry yellow,
and to that pink that only awe can indicate.

It sat for years so by the window,
whilom watered and relaxed;
one pot accumulating bulbs: winter ideas.

This time it came in spring
synchronous with humming green
and sparrow song, with morning light,
with hoarded imprints,
seed memories of many cold captivities.

Within the bands and courses
of all those gentle constellations
disappearing in the light of many mornings,
it says, "my love, please don't predict.
The year is long. And even summer
yields to many possibilities."

How We Got Our Name

The press is named for "Pleasure Boat Studio," an essay written by Ouyang Xiu, Song Dynasty poet, essayist, and scholar, on the twelfth day of the twelfth month in the renwu year (January 25, 1043):

> "I have heard of men of antiquity who fled from the world to distant rivers and lakes and refused to their dying day to return. They must have found some source of pleasure there. If one is not anxious for profit, even at the risk of danger, or is not convicted of a crime and forced to embark; rather, if one has a favorable breeze and gentle seas and is able to rest comfortably on a pillow and mat, sailing several hundred miles in a single day, then is boat travel not enjoyable? Of course, I have no time for such diversions. But since 'pleasure boat' is the designation of boats used for such pastimes, I have now adopted it as the name of my studio. Is there anything wrong with that?"
>
> *Translated by Ronald Egan*

About the Author

Walter Hess was born in Germany and emigrated, with his family, to the U.S. in 1940, via Ecuador. Educated in New York City schools with a BA from CCNY in 1952 and an MA from CCNY in 2003. He is a retired documentary film editor. Films on which he collaborated have won numerous awards, among them two Peabody's and three Emmy's. Metamorphoses has published his translations from the German of the poetry of Hans Sahl. In 2001 he received an award from The Academy of American Poets, and in 2003 a cash award from the Nyman Foundation for a portion of his memoir.

About the Illustrator

A professional graphic designer, Herb Stern worked most recently for Ziff-Davis, a media conglomerate specializing in computer information. He retired in 1999. His personal interests led him to painting and printmaking in various media including acrylics, oils, and watercolors. His printmaking involves photo images and drawing executed as etchings and lithographs. Exhibitions include solo shows at Fairleigh Dickinson University, The Interchurch Center in New York City, JCC on the Palisades, and numerous other New Jersey venues. He is a member of the Art Center Painting Affiliates which exhibits regularly in the tri-state area.